101 Ways

to Massively

Increase

the Value of Your Real Estate
without Spending Much Money

ISBN: 0-7835-7901-2

Printed in Canada
10 9 8 7 6 5 4 3 2 1

TIME
LIFE

Published by Time Life Direct.
TIME-LIFE is a trademark of Time Warner Inc.
and affiliated companies.

For information on and a full description
of other Time-Life products, please call 1-800-621-7026
or go to www.TimeLife.com

For information on and a full description
of other Dolf de Roos products,
please go to www.dolfderoos.com

101 Ways

to Massively

Increase

the Value of Your Real Estate
without Spending Much Money

Dolf de Roos

Real Estate Investor

Contents

Acknowledgments

The 101 ideas presented in this book come from many sources. Some were gleaned from discussions with fellow real estate investors, some from interactions with real estate agents, and some from my extensive reading of real estate books. Many I dreamed up in the shower, while dozing off to sleep, or on long-haul flights. Most have been tested on my properties, modified, adapted, refined, and then tried once more.

I would like to thank the countless real estate professionals (and amateurs) that I have come in contact with over the years with whom I have exchanged ideas. In particular I would like to thank my mentoring students with whom I regularly brainstormed ideas for massively increasing the value of real estate without spending much money. While just about anyone, when given the assignment of dreaming up ideas on improvements, thinks of painting the house, there are some less obvious gems that the mentoring students contributed to this eclectic collection that are equally valid and effective.

I would also like to thank Larry Jellen and Denise Dersin at Time Life Direct for believing so strongly in this project. You are not only true professionals, but fun to work with.

Introduction

In my best-selling book *Real Estate Riches*, I make the case that real estate is not just a little better than other investments, and not even just a lot better than other investments, but that it is in fact hundreds and even thousands of times better.

To do this, I compared real estate with other investments typified by stocks. I asked four simple questions, as follows:

1. If you have $100,000 cash to invest, how many dollars worth of stocks can you buy? The answer for most investors would have to be: "Exactly $100,000."

Conversely, if you have $100,000 cash to invest, how many dollars worth of real estate can you buy? Now the answer is more like $1 million, as you can easily get bank financing to fund the acquisition.

2. The day you buy your $100,000 worth of stocks, what is that portfolio worth? The answer has to be that, by definition, the stocks are worth exactly $100,000, as the stock market is very efficient, and someone in Cambridge, Massachusetts would pay the same price for a given stock at any given time as someone else in Boise, Idaho.

On the other hand, what would the property that you just paid $1 million for be worth? It may only be worth

$740,000 (someone talked you into paying too much for it—in other words you bought a lemon). By the same token, it may be worth $1.5 million, and you just bought yourself a bargain. The sale prices of real estate differ from the "true value" because the real estate market is very inefficient. Someone in Boise, Idaho may not have ready access to the details on a property in Cambridge, Massachusetts the way he or she would with paper assets. And then there are 101 reasons why someone would sell a property at way below its true market value. In the book *Real Estate Riches* I further explain why it is easier to buy a property under true value than above value (I called this the instant lemon-avoidance algorithm.)

4. I know I have skipped to number four. Here we said, assume that everything has doubled in value. What must you do to get some of the benefit of the increase in value of your stocks? The answer for most people is to sell some of them.

If your real estate doubled from $1.5 million to $3 million, what must you do to get some of the benefit of the increase in value? Clearly you could sell, but another option is simply to refinance, to go back to the banks with a new appraisal, and get even more money from them.

3. The question we skipped goes as follows: You bought stocks for $100,000 cash. The day you bought them, they were worth exactly $100,000. What can you personally do to increase the value of these stocks? The answers were very limited. You could hope, pray, write letters of encouragement to the officers of the company, and you could buy as many of the products and services of these companies as you could afford, hoping that the resulting increased turnover would increase the stock prices sufficiently to compensate your outlay.

Now let's pose the same question with regard to real estate. You bought a property for $1 million using $100,000 cash and a $900,000 mortgage. The day you bought it, it was really worth $1.5 million (in other words you bought a bargain). What can you personally do to massively increase the value of the property without spending much money?

My answer to this question has always been, "Wow! Where do we start?" There are dozens of ideas that come to mind straightaway. There are more that come to mind when you start thinking about it a little bit. There are ideas that my mentoring students have come up with, that people on my database suggest, and that I dream up in the middle of the night. There are easily 101 things you can do to massively increase the value of a property without spending much money! You could fill a book with ideas.

Well, this is that book. If you find it extensive, please remember that it is not the last word on improvements. The 101 ideas presented here are just a start. There were many more ideas that came to mind just in the process of getting these down on paper. There will be others that you dream up while reading these. There will be more ideas that we don't even know about yet because the technology is not yet here to facilitate them.

Keep in mind that any idea, once written down and explained, tends to seem obvious to a passive reader. In case you think that these 101 ideas are not very original, then I invite you to submit your own, new, original ideas through our website for everyone to be able to benefit from (details at the back of this book).

Overall, you are limited only by your imagination. One of the things I love about real estate is that once you have purchased a property, you can do many things to increase its value way more than the cost of making the improvement. What a perfect vehicle for turning thoughts into money—creating something out of nothing. This is the ultimate in alchemy.

Enjoy, and as always, successful investing!

Dolf de Roos

Section 1

Residential Real Estate

1. *The humble carport.*

One of my favorite examples of how to increase the value of
a property way beyond the cost of the execution concerns a
carport.

Imagine you have a residential investment property
that has neither a carport nor a garage. The tenant's car
must be left outside in the rain, sun, hail, sleet, and snow.

Surely it is reasonable to assume that, if you were to
provide a carport with this property, the value to the tenant
would go up. Now I know from experience that in many parts
of Australia, New Zealand, the United States, and Canada,
the additional rental that you can get by having a carport is
easily around $20 per week or $80 per month. In some places
it will be a bit less, and in others a bit more, but let's assume
that this is a reasonable increase in rental when you put in a
carport.

Now a carport is not a difficult structure to build. In its
most common form it comprises four poles and a roof with a
slope. If you want to be really cheap, you could get away with
three poles, but that would be silly. An outlay of $1,000 gen-
erally covers it.

With the carport in place, you should easily get an extra
$80 per month. This translates to an annual income from the
carport of around $1,000. In this case, the return on your
$1,000 investment would be 100% per annum. If you owned

such a residential investment property without a carport or garage, why would you not build one?

I do not know of any other investment vehicle other than real estate where you can easily spend an additional $1,000 and then get a massive 100% return on that extra investment per annum.

But our carport example doesn't stop there!

One option is to pay cash for the carport, and then receive a 100% return per annum. But this is how you could do even better:

Imagine you had the carport built. You haven't paid for it yet, so remember that we must still pay the $1,000. However, with the new rental in place, you call in an appraiser, and tell him you want an appraisal based on the fact that you now have increased your income by $1,000 per annum. With an extra income of $1,000, the value of the property is likely to go up by something like $10,000 (based on capitalizing the rental at 10%). With this new appraisal for $10,000 more, you can go back to the bank and get a new mortgage. Using a very modest 70% loan-value ratio, the bank will lend you $7,000 at an interest rate of, say 10%.

So now you have received $7,000 from the bank. Remember we still have to pay for the carport, so we use $1,000 of the $7,000 to pay the contractor. We also have to pay the bank annual interest of $700. Now we are receiving an extra $1,000 per annum, so after paying our mortgage interest, we are only left with $300 of annual income.

However, you still have $6,000 left in your pocket (the $7,000 mortgage, less the $1,000 to build the carport). Ask yourself this question: Is the $6,000 taxable? Well it certainly is not income, so no income tax is payable. And you didn't sell anything, so there can be no talk of a capital gains tax or of a sales tax. There are in fact no tax obligations on $6,000. This money has been created out of nothing!

Just to recap, you can either pay for your carport in

cash, and receive $1,000 per year indexed for inflation (a 100% return on your investment of $1,000). Or, you can pay nothing, receive $300 per year indexed for inflation and leveraged (an infinite return since you did not put up any capital) *and put $6,000 in your pocket on which there are no tax obligations.*

Either way, if you owned such a property, why would you not do it? And if you think that it is not worth it for a mere $1,000 per year, what if you had 20 such properties? Would you do it for $20,000 per year, or, using the second option, would you like to put $120,000 in your pocket tax free?

Now I can already hear the "Yes, but" brigade complain in protest: "Yes, but where I come from, you couldn't possibly build a carport for a mere $1,000." Look, even if it cost you $4,000 to build, that would still represent a cash-on-cash return of 25%, and using the second option, you would still be putting $3,000 in your pocket. Putting no cash into the $4,000 carport is still infinitely better than putting no cash into the bank!

2. *Turn a carport into a garage.*

Depending on how a carport is constructed, it may be an easy job to turn it into a fully enclosed garage. For instance, many houses continue their roofline beyond the end wall of the house, to provide the roof for the carport. Often there is a solid wall at the far end of the carport. In this case, enclosing the carport just involves putting a garage door on the front of the carport, between the end wall and the house, and enclosing the rear of the carport. Doing this has the added benefit that normally the square footage of a carport is not included in that of the house, but that of a walk-in garage often is.

3. *Turn a garage into a "sleep-out" or spare bedroom.*

Particularly in times of economic downturn, many people seek ways of accommodating more people (usually family members) at the same property. One favorite method has been to convert a freestanding garage into a spare bedroom. Usually the garage will already have electricity supplied to it, so that putting in adequate lighting and even a hot plate and microwave is relatively easy. Putting plumbing in to allow for a lavatory and hand basin or even a shower is a more ambitious undertaking, but once completed, can really increase the value of the real estate as there is now another source of income from it.

4. *Put up a new front fence.*

If there is no front fence, or if the existing fence is crooked, rotted, and dilapidated looking, then putting up a new front fence can instantly change the initial impression that most people (including the appraiser) will have of your house.

Depending on the nature of your property and the suburb it is in, you may want a low, picket fence to show off the front garden, or you may want a high, solid fence to block street noise, give privacy, and increase security. Either way, the fence is usually the first thing you see of a piece of real estate, so having it look great is very smart.

5. *Paint!*

I love the carport example, because it is so easy to conceptualize, easy to implement, and easy to be convinced of the financial benefits.

However, it is by no means the simplest thing you can do to massively increase the value of a property.

One of the easiest things you can do to massively increase the value of a property is to paint it, or better still, have someone paint it for you. In fact, there are dozens of things you can do with paint to give a real benefit beyond the cost of implementation, but I will lump them all together here so as not to have a big chunk of our 101 ideas hijacked by paint.

The most obvious starting point is to paint the outside of the house. In fact, if you are really cheap, you could just paint the front of the house, as that is the side that people will generally see first and will therefore give the most "bang for the buck." Just kidding, but seriously, painting the outside of the house can have a tremendous effect on the look and feel of the entire property. And don't just choose your paint at random, or based on whichever is the cheapest. The judicious choice of contemporary colors, or appropriate colors for the style and age of the house, will pay off handsomely. Furthermore, do not just swathe the entire house in one color: By choosing contrasting colors for the window sills and doors, shutters, and window frames, you can enhance the effect even further.

After considering the outside of the house, you may want to consider painting the roof. A fresh coat of paint on the roof can not only be excellent preventive maintenance, but will also greatly improve the look of the house.

Next you may want to paint the front fence, and then any other fences on the property. The old tool shed, carport, garage, mailbox, and other outdoor structures should not be forgotten either.

Inside the house, a room or hallway may be dark because the walls are painted or papered with a dark color. A fast solution is to paint them a lighter color. This will give a clean, airy feeling. A fresh coat of paint also covers a lot of blemishes such as fading around previous picture frames, pin and nail holes, scuff marks, and tape residues.

Ceilings may also benefit from a fresh coat of paint.

When it comes to closets and cupboards, remember that even though we do not normally look inside these, let alone live or work in them, when these spaces are freshly painted with a light color, it makes it easier to find things in them, and there is no reluctance to put anything inside them.

By the way, if you are considering doing the actual painting yourself, remember that there are more application methods than just using a paintbrush. Roller brushes are fast, efficient, and leave a good finish, while spray-painting equipment can be rented by the hour or for a day or two. I just don't recommend Mr. Bean's infamous paint-bomb method.

6. *Cut the grass.*

Before we even set foot inside the house or building on the property, there are many things you can do to dramatically increase the perceived value. One of the simplest (and this one is surprisingly often overlooked) is to cut the grass. Mow the lawns, for heaven's sake! I don't think that mowing the lawns so much increases the value, as much as leaving the lawns uncut degrades the value, but either way, I am always delighted to inspect real estate where the grass comes up to my waist, as I know that I can deduct thousands of dollars off the price (if the sellers or their agents have not already done so), even though the cost of cutting the grass may only be a couple of hundred dollars.

This concept of making thousands of dollars from cutting the grass was entrenched in my mind when I was still a student studying to get a Ph.D. in electrical and electronic engineering. Here I was, studying way more than 8 hours a day, bemoaning the fact that I was on a miserly student's stipend of $3,000 for the year (okay, it was a couple of decades ago), and complaining to anyone who would listen about the owners of the house next door who seemed to have vanished and left the exterior of the house and the garden to the elements. It was only after almost 18 months of this property being in this derelict state, that someone smarter than I bought this property, cut the grass, painted the exterior, and did a few other things like that, and then sold it for a profit equivalent to a lifetime of being on my student stipend. It was then that I realized that I had been a fool to have seen this opportunity at least once in the mornings when I left my home, and once again in the evenings when I returned, and not to have done something about it. Now of course I relish the rare find of a house badly in need of some serious grooming.

7. *Seal the driveway.*

For many people, a driveway is a driveway, and they never think about it. I also know of some people who, when I suggested that they seal their gravel driveway, looked horrified at the idea, retorting that the gravel was a great burglar deterrent as any car driving up the drive or person walking there, could easily be heard from inside the house.

That idea has some merit, but a gravel driveway also suffers from inherent disadvantages. For instance, weeds easily grow after a while, the gravel needs to be raked back in place, gravel finds its way onto your lawns so that individual stones become missiles when struck by the blades of your turbocharged lawn mower, and some of the gravel inevitably finds its way into the house. Furthermore, burglar deterrent value notwithstanding, they are noisy!

The solution is obvious. Seal the driveway. This alone will greatly improve the feel of the whole property.

8. *Put in a new letter box.*

In some places, the mail carrier comes right to the front door and delivers the mail through a letter slot in the door. In others, the mail is delivered to a cluster of letter boxes that service 20 or so homes. Usually, however, each home has a letter box somewhere near the street. Letter boxes are often made of cheap materials, which is why they deteriorate so quickly after just a few years of use. Furthermore, they are exposed to the elements all the time. It is not surprising that they look horrible in a very short space of time. Since a letter box can be one of the first things you notice about a property, spending $70 on a new letter box can reap disproportionately large rewards.

9. *Landscape.*

Having cut the grass, we may decide that doing some general landscaping will greatly affect the feel of the property. Landscaping can take many forms, from throwing a few stone slabs on the front lawn to make a pathway to the front door to bringing in bulldozers to create mounds and gullies. Remember to stay focused on the task at hand. We are not trying to make the best house we can to live in. Rather, we are trying to massively increase the value of the real estate without spending much money. Therefore, bringing the bulldozers in to make a moat around the buildings may not be cost-effective, apart from the fact that what you had hoped would look like a castle may to everyone else simply look like a bomb site.

Having said that, there is plenty of opportunity to use your imagination. Put in some flower beds, install a pergola, get rid of a slimy, leaking fishpond, or install a new fishpond, turn a vegetable garden into a grassed area, turn a grassed area into a lawn-tennis court, or allow a climbing plant to cover a not so desirable shed. The services of a landscape gardener may be money well spent here.

10. *Plant trees.*

Trees can turn an otherwise barren landscape into an aesthetically appealing oasis that provides shade from the sun, shelter from the wind, and a habitat for birds. Now if you merely planted seeds or seedlings, then notwithstanding the fact that the outlay would be very small, the time it would take to reap the benefit of your effort would be very long. What I am suggesting is that you pay to have mature trees delivered and "installed" on your property. Naturally this will cost a bit more, but if spending $2,000 on trees can increase the value by $10,000, then that is a good trade-off. Companies that provide this service exist—it's just a matter of tracking them down, and having the gumption to give it a try. You see city councils put in a whole row of trees along new boulevards or around new facilities, but the effects are just as dramatic when applied to your own properties.

11. *Remove trees.*

While I am generally much more in favor of planting trees than chopping them down, there are instances when existing trees can be a nuisance (obstructing access, leaving sticky residues, or blocking light to the inside of the building). And trees, being living things, do die. Sometimes a house can be improved tremendously just by getting rid of a dead, rotting tree in the front garden that is a real eyesore, or by trimming a tree that is restricting light and warmth to the living room.

12. *Replace the spouting.*

Rusty galvanized iron spouting, or cracked, sun-faded and broken plastic spouting can look terrible. Replacing the non-functioning eyesores with new spouting will reduce the maintenance requirements on the property, while at the same time increasing the value of the real estate way beyond the cost of the spouting. Because spouting is so visible, bad spouting is one of the first things noticed by potential buyers, tenants, and appraisers alike. Depending on the style and color scheme of the buildings in question, you may want to use white PVC spouting, or even the more upmarket copper spouting.

13. *Put up new curtains.*

While curtains are primarily used to prevent "unauthorized eyes" from peering into our homes during the hours of darkness, they also double as heat insulators (think of thermal drapes) and lighting control devices. Whether they are ever closed when the sun is shining outside or not, the sun still beats down on them most of the time, and curtains are therefore subject to phenomenal fading through ultraviolet light from the sun. One of the most dramatic improvements that you can therefore make to a house is to replace faded curtains and drapes.

If curtains are faded, that is a great reason to replace them. But even if they are not faded, replacement may still lift the feel of the property. For instance, the existing curtains may be hopelessly out of fashion (think of bright floral patterns from the 1960s), worn, torn, too short, too long, or not wide enough to cover the entire window space when they are drawn. In any of these cases, replacing the curtains with something more modern, in terms of color, style, suspension method, and materials, can deliver massive benefits way beyond the cost of the new curtains.

14. *Electrify the curtains.*

I am not talking about making your curtains part of your defense against burglars by electrocuting these uninvited guests should they come through the windows, although I am sure there is an opportunity in there somewhere. Rather, I am talking about installing electric curtain openers/closers. As with most items discussed in this book, the cost of implementing an idea like this is but a small fraction of the perceived value that it brings to the piece of real estate. Since having electric curtain openers is such a rare thing even today, most people, be they prospective tenants, purchasers, or appraisers, when they see such gadgetry installed and working smoothly will in their minds place an enormous premium on the real estate.

Furthermore, electric curtains can indeed still form part of your defense against burglars, as you can program the curtains to open at dawn and close at dusk, thereby fostering the illusion that you are at home, even if you are in Europe on vacation (assuming they do not all open and close at the exact same time, which would be a dead giveaway!)

15. *Stretch carpet if rippled.*

Very often, a carpet will look ruined when all that has happened is that it has stretched and left unsightly ripples running at random through the house. All that needs to be done in this case is to have a carpet layer stretch the carpet, taking up any slack.

16. *Steam clean carpets.*

While still on carpets, I have seen people spend a small fortune replacing carpets, when all that was really required was for the carpets to be steam cleaned. Carpet cleaning technology has improved greatly over the years, and you will be surprised how good a dirty carpet with stains, spots, and marks can be made to look again. It would be foolish to replace a carpet, if steam cleaning can achieve the desired effect.

17. *Replace carpets.*

Of course not all carpets just need to be stretched or cleaned. Where carpets have been worn beyond the point of redemption, then by all means one of the best things you can do to improve the look and feel of a house is to replace the carpets. And this need not be a costly exercise! Secondhand carpets in almost new condition can often be acquired at a fraction of the price of a new carpet. Similarly, if you go to factory outlets, you will often be able to pick up end-of-run carpets for a song.

18. *Get rid of the carpet altogether!*

As an alternative to stretching rippled carpets, steam cleaning dirty carpets, or replacing carpets that have been worn beyond redemption, you may want to check what is under the carpet. Especially in older houses, the floorboards can be of beautiful heartwoods. In this case, it may be best to rip the old carpet and padding out, have a commercial contractor come in to sand the floorboards, and then have them lacquered with polyurethane to provide a hardy finish. The effect can be dramatic, and you'll never have to replace the carpets again.

19. *New light fixtures and lampshades.*

Apart from carpets and curtains, one of the most telling signs of the age of a building is the style of the light fixtures and lampshades. Fortunately, these are also some of the easiest things to replace.

Early light fixtures were often made of Bakelite, which had the horrible side effect of emitting a foul odor when they got hot from the heat of the lamp. Replace them all! A visit to a modern lighting showroom will reveal all manner of lights and lamps for very modest prices.

Since light fixtures that hang down from the ceiling also make a room appear smaller, you may want to consider replacing suspended lights with those imbedded in the ceiling. Track lighting is useful if you have featured walls or hangings to highlight. Halogen lighting also has a different feel about it, so consider halogen lamps, especially for modern homes. Once again, for a relatively small outlay, you can dramatically improve the look and feel of a house.

20. *Replace the light switches.*

Initially you may wonder what on earth you could gain by changing a light switch. Well, quite a lot. First, some older light switches simply look old and feel dirty. More modern ones can help make a place look far more modern. Some even have neon lights imbedded in them to help you locate them when it is pitch dark. Alternatively, you may want to replace plastic switches with original or reproduction art-deco switches if these are more in keeping with the style of the home. For instance, such switches may have polished brass or carved wood faceplates.

Secondly, you may want to consider light dimmer switches. Older kinds have rotating knobs with which you can adjust the brightness, while more recent ones have touch pads which you touch briefly for instant ON or OFF, or touch for longer periods to have them dim up or down.

The last house we were in had very sophisticated electronic dimmers. There was instant ON to full brightness, and also instant OFF. However, once a brightness level had been set (as indicated by a vertical column of discrete green LEDs) you could then have the lights gradually dim down to nothing from this level, and, when you wanted the lights on again, you could have them gradually dim up to this level. It may sound like unnecessary gadgetry, but I will have to confess that once you have had them, you miss them when they are absent. For instance, if you needed to get up in the middle of the night for whatever reason, instead of having the lights either off or full on, and instead of manually dimming them up to the required level, you could simply touch the appropriate pad to have them gradually dim up to a very low level that was perfect for whatever got you up. These light dimmers worked perfectly, and looked the part too. Remember, a small thing like this on its own may not change the value of your real estate dramatically, but a whole succession of them may just convince everyone involved that you have a very special house.

The ultimate in house light switches would have to be one of the remote systems currently on the market, whereby you have a remote-control unit similar to a television remote control, where you can adjust the brightness of individual lights throughout your house, clusters of lights, or all of them together. With a remote in the car, you can turn on the lights before you enter the house, or conversely only turn them off after you leave. This system may be a bit extravagant for a small, two-bedroom rental on the cheap side of town, but for an upmarket executive house, the $1,200 or so installation cost could be recouped every year through extra rentals, and recouped instantly through extra borrowings against increased equity.

21. *Wash walls and ceilings.*

Many of the ideas we are considering in this book require you to buy something and then fit it to the house. Often all that a place needs is a bit of cleaning to bring it back up to standard. Washing the walls and ceilings, especially after smokers have been living in the house, can do wonders to the appearance, rental value, and appraisal of your real estate.

22. *Put in extra telephones.*

I am showing my age by revealing that when I was a kid, we had a grand total of one telephone in the house. It was located in the downstairs hallway, and if the phone rang, someone had to rush out from somewhere to answer it. Through my interest in electronics, our house soon became a telephone addict's delight, with phones conveniently located just about everywhere, notwithstanding the fact that we still had only one line.

With the advent of cordless telephones and multiple phone lines in homes (we currently have four incoming lines), the need for multiple phone jacks has diminished. However, many older rental units still have only one or two telephone jacks. One hundred dollars spent putting in a telephone jack in every bedroom, and putting phones at those locations, can be repaid many times over in increased value.

23. *Put clear house numbers on the house and somewhere in the street.*

If you travel around visiting people with any degree of regularity, you will share my view that very few homes have clearly visible house numbers on them. Therefore I propose that you put large numbers on both the house if it is visible from the street, and also somewhere on the street if it is allowed by local bylaws. For instance, you may paint the house numbers on the concrete guttering in many places, making it easy for taxis and visitors to find a particular house. You can also buy solar-powered street numbers that light up at night, making it even easier to locate a particular house. Once again, the cost involved is minute, but the perceived value can be much higher.

24. *Outside light at front door.*

As both a security measure and to make the arrival of guests and tenants alike more pleasant, a solid, bright light at or near the front door is always welcome. It could have a sensor on the path to turn the light on when someone approaches at night, but it should also have an override switch inside the house.

25. *Install big mirrors.*

Even if a house is not overly large to begin with, you can certainly create the illusion of space by installing large mirrors. While these may take the form of large, framed, hanging mirrors, it is becoming increasingly common to have an entire wall made of mirrors. The increase in perceived area, and the improvement in lighting, will have a beneficial effect on the tenants and the appraiser.

26. *Touch up all chipped corners.*

There is a general wear and tear in a house that comes about from daily living. Typically, edges around doors and doorframes get chipped as suitcases, strollers, boxes, and furniture gets moved about. When there is enough chipping, it can degrade the look of the entire house. An hour spent going around touching up all the chipped paint can do wonders.

27. *Hang new wallpaper.*

Some houses just do not do well with fresh paint—new wallpaper would be more appropriate to remain in keeping with the style of the property. If this is the case, do not hesitate. Old wallpaper, like old paint, shows the signs of fading, nail holes from pictures and paintings, and general discoloration. The cost of wallpapering will again be repaid many times over.

28. *Put in a skylight.*

Very often, older homes and premises will not have the generous allocation of windows that modern houses have. As a result, there will often be dark corners, areas, or even entire rooms. An inexpensive way of overcoming this is to install a skylight in the ceiling that allows daylight to pour in and thus illuminate the otherwise dark area. With the extra light, the building will seem larger, warmer, and more inviting. Needless to say, this increases its value.

If the area where you need more light is not directly covered by a roof that could accommodate a skylight, then you can get "solar-tubes" that channel the daylight from a point on the outside of the building to your dark area using flexible, insulated tubing. These are a bit more expensive to buy and install, but the result is the same.

Should the installation of a skylight or solar-tube be beyond your budget or inclination to do some work, then the next idea is for you.

29. *Replace the light bulbs with bulbs of much higher wattage.*

Replacing light bulbs with ones of higher wattage may seem sneaky, but maybe the original bulbs were installed by a cheapskate who had them underpowered to save a few dollars a year in electricity costs, leaving the building looking dark, dingy, and gloomy. Putting bright bulbs in place will generally put everyone in a better mood, will make the place look bigger and brighter, will make the place easier to rent or sell, and most interestingly for my line of work, will make the appraiser more inclined to think that it is a great property rather than a mediocre one. You can't get much better value for money than the value you will get out of a new set of light bulbs (and you get to keep the old ones, if that matters to you).

30. *Install a garbage disposal unit in the kitchen sink.*

A generation ago a garbage disposal may have seemed a luxury, but these days more and more people wonder how they even managed without one. Once again, the cost of installing this kitchen gadget will be recouped many times over in terms of increased property value.

31. *Install a dishwasher.*

Just as with the garbage disposal unit, a dishwasher is a modern convenience that few of us can imagine being without, while a generation ago they were not that common at all. Nonetheless, if you come across a piece of real estate that is not yet equipped with a dishwasher, then installing one has multiple benefits. You will be able to attract tenants at a much higher rental level, you can depreciate the acquisition, and the value of the real estate (against which you can borrow money) will have gone up.

32. *Install a range hood.*

While garbage disposal units and dishwashers are becoming common items in modern homes, range hoods to suck away cooking fumes are still a rarity in many regions. The benefits should be pretty self-evident in terms of odor extraction, and yet I don't know of anyone else who has ever retrofitted range hoods to homes that they already own. Can you see how with just the addition of these last three items, your kitchen will start to seem quite modern?

33. *Change the stove!*

Many rental units have cooking stoves that seem to date from the middle ages, with the old-style spiral elements on them (that collect and burn food). I even know landlords who, when a stove needs replacing, scour the secondhand shops to buy an old replacement stove for $50 or so, and then they ask me why their tenants were not ecstatic with their solution! Get with it. First, stoves can generally be depreciated at a much higher rate than other personal property items. Secondly, if the cook of the household comes along for the initial property inspection, then the stove will be about the first thing looked at. Thirdly, the property will appraise at a sufficiently higher value to make the purchase worthwhile.

34. *Remodel the entire kitchen.*

Depending on the condition of the kitchen, simply installing a garbage disposal unit, dishwasher, range hood, and new stove may be enough to change it from a great kitchen to a fabulous kitchen. However, if the kitchen is pretty horrible to start with, then putting in those four new items will just make the rest of it look like what it is: sorely in need of a remodeling job.

So, why not give the kitchen a complete makeover? There are companies around that specialize in installing complete new kitchens. Sometimes they are prefabricated. Sometimes they are made to measure in the factory and then installed in your home. And sometimes they are custom made at your home. Either way, they will give you new cupboards, counters, dual sinks, multifunction taps, utilitarian lighting, storage units, functional garbage containers and compacting systems, cutlery and crockery holders, refrigeration systems, microwave ovens, appliance garages, power outlets, and easy to clean flooring. Such kitchens may cost from $10,000 to $30,000, but in almost each case, the value of the real estate will go up by much more than the expenditure. And remember, the expenses can be depreciated, the rental value will go up, the ease with which you can find tenants will go up, their reluctance to move on will go up, your equity will increase, and your net worth will go up. Talk about a win-win situation!

35. *Remodel the bathroom.*

Now that we are in the mood for remodeling, the other room to consider for a complete makeover is the bathroom. Kitchens and bathrooms are generally the two rooms that most reveal the age of a property. However, do not rush into modernizing a bathroom: While most people wouldn't ever want to have to cook on an old coal range, there is a nostalgic plus in the old freestanding iron tubs standing on metal claws.

Having said that, however, old bathrooms, with separate hot and cold water faucets that are so close to the basin that you cannot rotate your hands freely underneath them to perform that simplest of bathroom tasks of washing one's hands, a single light bulb in the center of the bathroom, and a single, small mirror by the door, are from the last millennium. Therefore, in remodeling the bathroom, depending on space, make sure that there is a his and a hers basin, with the hot and cold water taps feeding a single mixed outlet, with large mirrors and plenty of lighting. Large mirrors are not only useful for monitoring one's progress at trying to look presentable for the day, but also increase the perception of space inside the bathroom, reflect the light more, and give the whole room an airy feeling.

Modernizing bathrooms and kitchens is the fastest way to add value to real estate, because so many of our waking hours are spent in them doing repetitive things where a slight increase in efficiency is greatly noticed.

36. *Build an extra bedroom.*

Let's assume that you have had a tenant in a particular house for a number of years. He has been a great tenant, always paying the rent on time, and looking after your property as if it were his own. Suddenly he comes to you to tell you that he must move on. Naturally, you inquire why, and he responds that his wife is pregnant again, and since the three-bedroom house they are renting from you will be too small for a family with three children, they very reluctantly need to move on.

You could just shrug your shoulders and figure out how to find a new tenant, hoping that they will be as good as the outgoing ones. Or, you could engage the existing tenant in some conversation. You could ask him if he would prefer to stay if it were not for the family expansion. If so, then why not make him an offer. Let's assume that three-bedroom houses in this area rent for $1,800 per month, whereas four-bedroom houses rent for $2,200 per month. Ask him if he would be willing to pay $2,200 per month for your house if you built an extra bedroom. Chances are he will have to pay this much for a four-bedroom house somewhere else, and by not shifting, he has no moving expenses, no changes of address to worry about, no new schools for the older children, and so forth. He is likely to say yes.

You may well ask, how can you afford to build an extra bedroom if you only get $400 a month for it? If it costs $30,000 to build such a bedroom, then it would take 75 months to pay off, or over 6 years.

Well, here is my reasoning. The extra revenue of $400 per month is equivalent to $4,800 per year. If we used that to pay interest on a loan, then at a generous 10% interest, you could service a loan of $48,000. We only need to borrow $30,000. What's more, the interest is tax deductible, whereas the capital outlay of $30,000 can be depreciated. If the value of the property goes up by a modest $40,000 with the addition of the bedroom, and we borrow $30,000 against that at

10% interest per annum, then we have increased our net rental income by $1,800 per year ($4,800 rental income less the $3,000 mortgage interest, assuming interest-only), we have increased our net worth by $10,000 ($40,000 increase in property value less the $30,000 mortgage), and we have the thanks and gratefulness of longstanding tenants.

That is why for me, when a tenant wants to leave, I see it as an opportunity for making him very happy and increasing my own net worth, equity, collateral, and passive income.

37. *Build an entire in-law apartment.*

While we are in the building mood, why not build an entire separate unit, complete with bedroom, small kitchen, bathroom, and lavatory. Of course you would have to check that such an undertaking is within the bounds of local regulations, but assuming that it is, then you have turned the house into what is often called a "home plus income." For the owners of such a property who live in the main house, having an in-law apartment can provide an income stream to help offset mortgage interest and other expenses. For an investor, the apartment represents a second, separate source of income from the property, dramatically improving returns (you did not have to buy the land as you already owned it).

38. *Subdivide the land and sell it off.*

If a piece of land is large enough, then it will be an easy matter to have the land surveyed, subdivided, and sold off. Doing so contravenes one of my Golden Rules as described in *Real Estate Riches*, namely Seldom Sell. However, if you are going to do nothing with the land otherwise, and if it will just cost money to maintain, then selling off would be an option. However, if you did have enough land to subdivide, then I would suggest the following.

39. *Subdivide the land and build on it.*

Let's assume that you purchased a piece of real estate as an investment in the past. Hopefully it would have been a good investment as is. However, if the land is large enough to allow you to subdivide, or if since buying the real estate the regulations have changed, so that you can now subdivide where before you couldn't, then you have a great opportunity to acquire another house, effectively without having to pay for the land.

The reason why I say you effectively do not have to pay for the land is that to you as an investor, the rental value of the original house will hardly be affected by the subdivision. If the original house was a four-bedroom villa generating $1,600 per month in rental, then it will probably still generate the same $1,600 per month after the subdivision. From an owner-occupier's point of view, it may be worth a lot less with half the land missing, but from a tenant's point of view, surplus land usually just means extra work on weekends.

Once you have legally subdivided the land, you can then go about having a house or unit built on it. Whatever you end up doing, it has to be better than starting off by buying vacant land on the open market. Sometimes we are sitting on a gold mine without even knowing it.

40. *Change the doorknobs.*

After remodeling the kitchen and bathroom, putting in an extra bedroom, adding an in-law apartment, subdividing our land, and building an extra house, it's time to move on to some simpler ideas!

Often, those items in a house that show the most wear and tear are those items that are touched, handled, and twisted most often: the doorknobs. Painted doorknobs can have paint chipped or worn off, coated metal handles can lose their coating, and all kinds can get loose, rattle, and appear dirty.

A couple of hundred dollars can generally go a long way toward replacing all the doorknobs and handles in a rental property, and the improvement can be dramatic. This is simple and quick to implement, and sure beats having the appraiser reluctant to open doors because the doorknobs seem so unpleasant.

41. *Replace the front door.*

Replacing all the doors in a house is a big exercise that is not usually warranted. However, if the front door is unsightly, worn, broken, or afflicted with panes of colored glass, or, worse still, frosted glass with designs in it as was the rage in the 1960s, then by all means replace the front door. Most people's first entry into a house is through the front door, so having this looking good is of great benefit.

42. *Add window screens.*

Window screens can be really wonderful, especially in areas with high numbers of insects, or annoying insects like sandflies or mosquitoes. They can be fitted over both doors and windows, so that you may still have a breeze blowing through the house. The screens that we have just had fitted coil away on a spring-loaded coil system, so that when not in use they are not in the way.

43. *Install security lighting.*

I remember as a kid, driving with my father in the country in New Zealand, when our car broke down. We walked to the nearest farmhouse. Not only was the key in the front door, but the door was wide open. We called out for someone, and when no one replied, walked down the hallway to the telephone. We called the operator (young readers will have to ask an older person what an operator is), told her of our predicament, and admitted that we were not even quite sure where we were. She told us we were at "James and Mary's house," and she knew that they were out for the afternoon, but she would phone around to see if any neighbors could help us out. She did, and they did. The whole point is that at no stage at all did either my father and I, or the operator, or the neighbors that helped us, ever think that we were doing something morally wrong by entering the house to use the telephone. The tacit assumption was that under slightly different circumstances, James and Mary would have felt they could take the same liberty at our house. Clearly these were the days before "security lighting."

Given that times have changed, however, security lighting is great to install on your properties. Activated by the infrared emissions from humans, these lights turn on when people get within a certain distance of their sensors. They are not only great as burglar deterrents, but are also useful when you arrive home after dark, as the lights will turn on to make your entry all the easier. Remember, an appraiser, in trying to figure out a fair value for your property, will take all these items into consideration. For an outlay of a couple of hundred dollars, the value may well go up by a couple of thousand.

44. *Install a burglar alarm.*

A much stronger deterrent for burglars is the presence of a burglar alarm (about the last thing a burglar wants is to be caught). Often, alarm companies will install a burglar alarm at very little cost or no cost at all, just to get the service contract. Ironically, the monthly fee of the service contract is usually paid for by the tenant. In other words, you can have a burglar alarm installed for nothing, the tenant feels a lot more secure, and the value of your property has gone up again, as the property is now "fully alarmed and monitored by a nationwide alarm company." Why would you not do it?

45. *Fire detection.*

Many burglar alarms include a fire detection module, setting off an alarm within the house in case of fire, and also sending a signal to the monitoring company (in case you are not at home to hear the alarm). However, in cases where the burglar alarm does not include such a module, or if there is not a burglar alarm to start with, then you can install fire detectors for a price that is so ridiculously low that you would have to be exceedingly arrogant not to protect yourself and your loved ones with several of these devices. These fire detectors cost less than $20, and last up to 5 years on a single titanium battery. Tenants will appreciate their presence, and appraisers will take them into consideration when forming their opinion of the worth of the real estate.

46. *Fire extinguishers.*

Fire detection is one thing, but having some tools to deal with a fire is a useful addition to a good fire detector. A good fire extinguisher placed in the kitchen, unobtrusively if such a gadget is considered an eyesore, should give you as landlord the confidence to know that even if there is a fire, there is at least a chance that the fire may be put out. Similarly, it gives the tenant the notion that you care enough about him and the property to provide one, and it gives him the chance to be able to save the day should the occasion arise.

47. *Install a decent set of locks.*

No matter how much is spent on building a home, most people skimp when it comes to installing locks. Door locks exist and are still sold for which there is only a limited number of *numbered* keys. Most locks are so flimsy in terms of design, materials used, and construction, that they can be breached in no time at all.

In the face of this, installing high-grade security locks sets you apart in the eyes of prospective tenants and appraisers alike. Let it be known that the keys for these locks cannot simply be copied at the local hardware store, but need to be taken to a registered locksmith who has to verify your right to copies. It is a way of announcing that you think that what's inside the house is worth more than average. Therefore, don't be surprised if through this mechanism, your appraiser will agree with you. And the cost of these locks for the front door, back door, and a side door may be under $200.

48. *Security doors.*

Speaking of increased security, a simple addition is to install so-called security doors. These are metal framed doors with a see-through mesh that are fitted over the outside of the normal front door, so that when someone knocks at your door, you can open your solid, normal front door first and see who is there, before unlocking the security door. Elderly people in particular seem to like these doors as an added level of protection.

Recently I was looking at a cluster of eight four-plexes, or 32 units in all. The quote for fitting security doors came in at $30 each. You can rest assured that the value of the units increased by way more than the $30 cost of fitting the doors.

49. *Plantation shutters.*

Plantation shutters are small wooden louvers set in latticework so that opening one opens a whole column simultaneously. They evoke a certain era and are often preferred to curtains as they are less dusty and can be set to keep out the sun without blocking the light altogether. Depending on the style of your house, plantation shutters have to be a great investment.

50. *Automatic lights inside closets.*

If you have ever had automatic lights inside cupboards, wardrobes, and closets, then you will not want to be without them again. The lights themselves make things so much easier to find or put away, while having them come on automatically when you open the closet door means you never have to fumble around for the switch, and you can never forget to turn them off again either. Here too there is a great ratio of perceived benefit to cost of installation.

51. *Insulation.*

Most people think of insulation with regard to heat insulation (namely keeping the house warm on the inside when it gets cold outside). However, in Phoenix, Arizona, for instance, you go to as much trouble to keep the desert heat *outside* the house. Either way, the methods to insulate the house are very similar.

The best way to ensure maximum insulation is to fit the insulating materials during the original construction of the building, when foam or fiberglass panels can easily be placed between walls and in the ceiling. However, if an older house is not well insulated, there are many things you can do to retrofit good insulation. Polyurethane expanding foam can be squirted through small holes in wall cavities. Drafts under a house can be reduced by sealing nonessential cavities. There are paints available now that have heat-reflecting properties, making them ideal for painting the insides of roofs to keep warmth in at night or during the winter, and to keep the heat out during the day or during the summer.

Of all the ideas presented in this book, providing good insulation is probably the least visible. However, you would be surprised how much extra renters or buyers are willing to pay to have a well-insulated house that may save them two or three hundred dollars worth of heating bills every year. Once again, the value may go up by much more than the cost of providing this insulation.

52. *Install double-glazed windows.*

Another improvement related to insulation is to double-glaze the windows. Not only does this provide excellent heat insulation, but it also provides tremendous sound insulation, and so is particularly recommended for houses or apartments that are in noisy environments such as those close to traffic or in busy cities. In addition to providing heat and sound insulation, however, double-glazed windows also virtually eliminate the problems of condensation that plague so many houses in colder climates. They also have the effect of making it difficult to see into your house from outside, at least during the daytime, giving you somewhat more privacy than ordinary windows.

Replacing all the glass panes inside a house with double-glazed windows will not be an inexpensive exercise. However, if you do your numbers beforehand, it could well turn out to be a lucrative improvement.

By the way, if you think that double glazing sounds like overkill, I have stayed in homes in Sweden where triple glazing is the norm, on account of the extreme cold. Strive to be a trend-setter, not a trend-follower.

53. *Install laminated windows.*

For heat insulation, it is difficult to beat double-glazed windows. However, if noise insulation is the desired outcome, then new forms of laminated glass windows claim to have an even higher noise suppression ability than double-glazed glass. Thus, for particularly noisy environments, check them out. They also have superior impact resistance to such things as wayward tennis balls from the neighbors to deranged drunks that gate-crash your tenants' parties.

54. *Enlarge the windows.*

Whether or not you want to put in double-glazed or laminated windows, there is merit in enlarging existing windows, especially those facing south in the Northern Hemisphere, and north in the Southern Hemisphere. Doing so will increase the ability to capture the heat of the sun, and will provide for much better lighting inside during daylight hours.

55. *Install sunshades.*

Conversely, where there is so much sun that heat is a problem, then a viable option is to provide shade from the sun. In Phoenix, Arizona, which gets notoriously hot during the nine months of summer, we have mesh screens that we affix to the outsides of our windows to help block the sun from entering the house, in addition to the more conventional style awnings that we can wind down over some of the windows.

56. *Add shutters to the sides of windows.*

Wooden shutters are common in Europe. For the most part, they are functional, blocking the sun during the summer, providing added darkness at night, and giving a measure of protection during storms. In many other parts of the world, wooden shutters on the sides of windows are not functional, but just serve as a decoration. There is nothing wrong with that—a flower bed is not very functional either.

When I bought the funeral parlor discussed in more detail later in this book and described in other publications, it was a plain building with little appeal. One of the first things that we did (I say we, as the tenant organized it, and I paid for it) was to have wooden shutters made and affixed to the sides of all the windows. The improvement in the way the property looked was dramatic, and no doubt contributed to the appraisal coming in at $280,000 even though I had effectively only paid $170,000 net for the property.

57. *Electric vertical shutters.*

In western Europe, especially in Belgium and France, it is very common for windows to have metal shutters that can be wound down to cover the entire window. They operate a bit like small versions of roller doors for garages. Initially these were all activated by hand from within the house, but newer ones are motorized. Apart from offering almost total darkness when they are pulled down, they are great for providing protection during storms, for securing the property when you are away on vacation, and for keeping the summer heat out of the house. Older people in particular seem to like the security these shutters offer, so if that is your demographic market, they are worth considering.

58. *Add a sun deck or convert an existing deck to a porch.*

A wooden sun deck or patio can add tremendous visual appeal and expand the amount of space available for indoor-outdoor living. It is a place to sit and chat in the sun, have barbecues, and sip drinks. If treated timber is used, then the boards will not tend to rot or warp. Like the front fence, this is one of the most noticeable things you can to do improve a property.

You could further enhance the patio by building a roof over it and putting in some railing, so as to turn the patio into a porch. In fact, you could turn the porch into a sunroom by glassing in the walls, and then start the process over by building a sun deck outside the sunroom. You are truly limited only by your imagination.

59. *Power wash the exterior of the house.*

Whether a house is made of wood, bricks, stone, shingles, stucco, or any other kind of cladding, the outside can end up looking old and tired from dust, dirt, grime, pollution, moss, and lichens. One cheap, quick, and easy thing to do to get rid of all the unsightliness is to power wash the exterior. You can rent power-washing equipment or get someone to do it for you. Either way, the results will be well worth your while.

60. *Clean roofing tiles of moss.*

Depending on the climate you are in, tiled roofs can develop moss. Having someone come periodically to power wash the moss off the roof can do wonders to the look of the house.

61. *Re-roof.*

If a roof is in a bad state of repair, then replacing the roof can also do wonders. What is more, if you replace a corrugated iron roof with tiles of some sort, then you will be adding extra value to the property, again massively increasing the value of the property beyond the cost of the improvement.

62. *Put in a trellis.*

Should there be something hideous that can be seen from your house, a simple solution is to add a trellis to your fence, thereby blocking the undesirable view. A trellis may also be a solution if your house is close to the neighbors' and you do not particularly want to be able to see what they are cooking for dinner (or, for that matter, have them see what you are cooking).

Even if there is no view that you wish to block, putting up a trellis or other framing for climbing plants to grow can improve the look of a house tremendously. What is more, as the climbing plants grow over time, the benefits of this simple improvement will keep on increasing.

63. *Put in a barbecue area.*

Whether or not you or your tenants end up using a barbecue very often, the mere presence of a barbecue area evokes images of happy family afternoon get-togethers and cool drinks on summer afternoons. For this reason alone, a barbecue is a good improvement investment. Furthermore, it can add a sorely needed feature to an otherwise dull backyard.

64. *Fit a shower over a bathtub if there is no shower.*

Most new homes are built with several bathrooms, most of which sport a shower. However, in the past, old homes tended to have just one bathroom, and as the name suggests, this was the room where the bathtub was—sans shower. Now to install a freestanding shower in an existing home is not always easy on account of the space required, but fitting a shower over an existing bathtub is a relatively simple matter. Suddenly, the home changes from having a bathtub to having a bathtub and shower.

65. *Install exhaust fans in bathrooms.*

Talking about bathrooms, until recently, few came equipped with an exhaust fan to take away the steam from showers. Consequently, ceilings and walls readily become moldy and discolored. Installing an exhaust fan is quick, easy, and cheap, and gives a very modern impression.

66. *Air conditioning.*

In some locations, it would be almost impossible to lead a normal life without an air-conditioning system. However, that does not mean to say that in less extreme climates, an air-conditioning unit would not be welcome at least during the summer.

The Japanese in particular have perfected the art of making small, efficient, and easy to install air-conditioning systems sized for a single room right through to an entire house. Having such a system readily adds more value to your house than the cost of installation.

67. *Reverse-cycle heat pumps.*

Even better than units that only provide air conditioning, are units that can either take heat from inside the house and dump it outside (cooling) or that can take heat from outside and dump it inside (heating). These units are often referred to as reverse-cycle heat pumps, as the heat can be pumped in either direction.

In many locations you only need heating, and in others, cooling may be all that is required. However, I can think of many places where it gets very hot in the summer and very cold in the winter. The extra money spent to acquire the reverse-cycle system will be well rewarded.

68. *Convert from leasehold to freehold land.*

Discussing the relative merits of freehold land (where you own the land and buildings) and leasehold land (where you own the buildings, but lease the land from someone else) could fill an entire book, especially if we went into the history of how the two categories came about.

Briefly, since you cannot depreciate land for taxation purposes, then when you buy leasehold land, you can depreciate the entire purchase price. Furthermore, the rental on the land tends to be reviewed only every seven years, or every 21 years. Therefore, in rent review year, you can expect to pay a fair market rental on the land, but for the subsequent six years (or 20 in the latter case), you will be paying a discounted rental relative to market rentals. These advantages are substantial.

Conversely, at the end of each lease period, you may not be able to renew the lease, and not only will you lose the right to use the land, but you may be required to remove all your buildings from the land. That is a huge disadvantage!

Having said all that, because leasehold land is so poorly understood, most people shy away from buying leasehold land, and as a result, leasehold real estate tends to sell at a discount to freehold land beyond the obvious differential from not owning the land itself. However, this creates an opportunity for the astute investor.

Sometimes it is possible to convert leasehold land into freehold land, by buying out the lessor of the land. Thus, if you buy leasehold land which is discounted because of the leasehold stigma, and then convert it to freehold, you will often find that you have paid much less for the resulting freehold real estate than if you had bought a comparable piece of real estate that was freehold from the outset.

69. *Put telephone and power lines underground.*

Sometimes the most beautiful homes are blighted by unsightly telephone and power cables crossing through the air on their way to these houses. If such is the case with any of your houses, see if you can have the cables put underground at the point of entry into your property. The improvement will be dramatic.

Often a whole suburb will be blighted by these cables. When we lived in La Jolla, California, we had to wind our way down a relatively steep street for about a mile from the top of the hill to La Jolla Corona Drive. The views of the deep blue of the Pacific Ocean were simply stunning, except that they were marred by literally dozens and dozens of thick, black cables spanning the street every 30 or 40 yards. In cases like these, lobby for your local authority, council, or county to have the cables put underground. Most communities have a program of putting telephone and power cables underground, and if you can hasten the process on your street, why not?

70. *Install a closet organizer.*

Even with the best intentions, closets tend to get messy quickly. That is why a modern closet organizer can be very appealing. These are systems with easy-roll drawers, baskets on rollers, swivel shelving, and efficient storage gadgetry for everything from shoes, belts, and ties to hats and shawls. It's one of those items like a dishwasher and remote garage door opener, that once you have had one, it is difficult to go back to not having one.

71. *Change from septic tank to sewer lines.*

These days, when a developer creates a subdivision for new houses, it is a requirement to provide running water, electricity, phone cabling, and a connection to the sewage system. However, in the past, these connections were not always obligatory and, as a result, homes can still be found where there is no connection to a sewage line. Instead, these homes had what is known as a septic tank.

Now, most investors, when they hear that a house has a septic tank, shy away from considering the property, as the whole concept is unfamiliar and ever so slightly disgusting, and it is easier to move on to the next potential investment. As a result, houses with a septic tank tend to sell at a discount.

Once again, the lack creates an opportunity. If you have or acquire such a house, spend the money to connect it to the sewage lines and remove the septic tank, and the house will no longer sell at a discount. So long as the cost of the changeover is much less than the increase in value, you are making money. And remember, you do not have to do the actual work yourself! You are making money by dreaming up ideas (or implementing the ones you read about here) and making phone calls.

72. *Install a videophone at the front door.*

Optical peepholes to see who was outside your door first became popular in hotels, but have since gained favor in homes as well. However, with the cost of video-intercoms being as low as they are, why not install a videophone at your front door? When someone pushes the doorbell, the television screen at your end automatically turns on to show who is there, and you can converse with them before deciding whether or not to even open the door to let them in. Most also have a facility for remotely opening the front door.

73. *Install a CCTV system in an apartment building.*

An idea I first came across at an apartment building in Houston, Texas was to have a series of closed-circuit television cameras at strategic locations around the apartment, such as in the parking garage, at the main entrance, and at the elevator doors. The signals from these cameras were fed to the distributed cable system throughout the apartment building, so that every apartment dweller could see the images on their television. Notices made it clear that the signals were distributed in this manner. Now on the one hand, I did feel as though people's privacy was somewhat invaded (you couldn't do anything without that nosey-parker down the hall knowing about it!). On the other hand, a person with ill intent would have to think twice, knowing that whatever he did, even his mere presence could be noted by any of dozens of potential witnesses.

Tenants tend to like this facility, and if crime were to go down as a result, then insurance premiums and/or deductibles (also called excesses) may go down. Overall, your building gets a really modern feel to it, and once again the value can go up by much more than the cost of installing the system.

74. *Install an electric garage door opener.*

This one should be a no-brainer. If your house still sports a manually operated garage door, put a remote-controlled electric door opener on it, or if that is not possible on the kind of door you have, replace the whole thing.

For years as a student, I had a garage without a remote door opener on it. If it was fine weather, I did not really mind getting out to open the door. (As an aside, I think it is ironic that we work day and night to buy laborsaving appliances, and then end up going to the gym because we get absolutely no exercise. Seen in this light, getting out of a car to open a garage door is great exercise!) However, when it rained, especially when it rained heavily, I cursed the fact that there was no remote opener. I should simply have installed one! Anyway, that was last century. Make sure you have joined the 21st century by ensuring all your garage doors have remotes on them.

75. *Electric baggage lifts.*

One of the delights of extensive travel is that you get to see great ideas that may be common in one geographic area, even though they may be almost unheard of anywhere else.

One idea that comes to mind is baggage, luggage, and grocery lifts that many holiday homes in the Marlborough Sounds of New Zealand have installed by their jetties. Many of these houses have no street access, and can only be reached by boat. While there are paths up from the jetties to the houses, they are not always well formed, and anyway, bringing a boatload of clothing, supplies, and groceries up these paths is not ideal. So, what many people have put in place are simple, winch-operated baggage lifts that run on rails of one sort or another. Groceries and other items are placed in the box or cart at the bottom, which is then winched up to the house.

Now this is not an idea likely to be suitable to many homes, but on the off chance that it could apply to one of your investments, it could really make the difference for a tenant who would otherwise not rent your property because he felt that the weekly chore of bringing up the groceries, firewood, dry cleaning, and parcel deliveries, not to mention taking out the garbage, was too much to be bothered with.

76. *Install extra electric outlets.*

Houses built more than around 50 years ago bear witness to the fact that there were not many electric-powered appliances around in those days. Whereas today we have radios, televisions, stereos, DVD players, VCRs, satellite receivers, cable boxes, cable modems, DSL modems, computers, monitors, cell phones to charge, digital still and video cameras to charge, humidifiers, dehumidifiers, night-lights, fans, cordless phones, fax machines, and so on and so forth, back then, it seems as if one electric outlet per room was considered adequate.

Consequently, if you find yourself with a house that has such a dearth of outlets, do yourself a favor by paying to have a whole slew of them installed.

77. *Ground fault circuit interrupters.*

Most electric outlets in houses are simply sockets that accept the plugs from our lamps and appliances such as televisions, toasters, and computers. Early power outlets had no switches on them, so that often you could see blue sparks as appliance plugs were inserted into them. Newer sockets have switches incorporated in them, some with neon lights to let you know when the outlet is powered and when it is turned off. Certainly, replacing the old, unswitched outlets with the newer switched ones makes everything look more modern.

However, until recently, there were essentially no power outlets in bathrooms. The reason is that there was always a risk that if the active or phase wire on an appliance was ever exposed, and you came into contact with it, then you could easily get electrocuted as your body would act as a conductor of the current.

In recent years, new outlets have become available that monitor the current leaving the active or phase wire, and compare it with the current being returned to the neutral wire. If there is ever a discrepancy, this would indicate that not all the current is being returned through the wires, which could mean that some is going through your body. Within less than a thirtieth of a second, these ground fault circuit interrupter power outlets switch themselves off, saving you from a potentially harmful electric shock.

Consequently, it is now possible to have all manner of appliances in a bathroom, such as hair driers, electric shavers, heat lamps, curling irons, ultrasonic jewelry cleaners, electric toothbrushes, and waterpicks.

Equipping your bathrooms with ground fault circuit interrupter power outlets will be money well spent. While these electronic outlets are much more expensive than their non-electronic counterparts, a couple of hundred dollars spent buying them and having them installed will reap huge rewards.

78. Give a tenant free, unlimited long-distance phone calls.

Often, the perceived value of something to a tenant may be more than the cost to you of providing it. Such is the case with long-distance phone calls or toll calls. Most tenants would jump at the chance of not having to pay for their long-distance calls, and yet the cost to you as landlord may be very little. Despite the low cost, it could increase rentals by far more than the cost of providing the long-distance calls, which in turn could increase the value of the property beyond what it would have been worth without this high-tech and invisible (at least non-tangible) addition.

79. Free, unlimited internet access.

In a similar vein to providing free and unlimited long-distance telephone calls, providing unlimited high-speed internet access is a very smart way of luring not only more tenants than the opposition, and at higher prices than they can charge, but you will also (tend to) get a smarter kind of tenant—those for whom high-speed internet access actually means something. Again, the financial benefits to you of providing this facility can be many times more than the cost of providing it.

For instance, my public company Property Ventures Limited is in the process of converting old commercial buildings into upmarket student accommodation. When we invited students along to a preliminary meeting to find out what sorts of things students would want in their apartment-style units, they were very receptive to the phone and internet ideas, to the extent that an unofficial waiting list was formed by these students—long before we even started work on the building conversions. The presence of this waiting list in all probability had some bearing on the appraisal or valuation of the project, which in turn would have helped with the finance application

Section 2

Commercial Real Estate

Without trying to sound trite, a whole book could be devoted to the things you can do to massively increase the value of commercial real estate without spending much money. However, since I know many real estate investors want to or are in the process of migrating from investing in houses to investing in commercial real estate, I want to include my favorite ideas for commercial real estate in this book.

80. *Fill empty buildings.*

With most commercial real estate, the value is not so much determined by the inherent worth of the land and buildings, but by the income-generating capacity of the property. The income is generally *capitalized* to arrive at the value of the real estate. Thus, a property generating $1 million a year in net income, using a capitalization rate of 10%, will be worth $10 million, even if the land only cost $345,000 and the building cost only $2 million to erect.

Thus, the simplest and fastest way to massively increase the value of a commercial property is to find a tenant for a vacant portion of the real estate.

I have applied this technique many times. In 1989 I came across a vacant funeral parlor. For those who may never have thought about such a building, a funeral parlor tends to have a viewing room, a slumber room, a chapel, a chilling room (no marks for guessing what they keep cool in there), and a mortuary with channels along the floor to drain fluids. It is probably fair to say that most people do not find it interesting to dwell on what goes on inside.

That is probably why the property had been vacant for some time. To me, however, it was also an opportunity. I had someone phone every funeral director in the country, to see if they wanted to expand into this town. Many of them dismissed the inquiry gruffly, but one funeral director said something like "I've always wanted to move into that town."

We ended up signing a legal agreement, under which he would become my tenant subject to me acquiring the property. Now I would like you to think about this for a moment. If I didn't manage to acquire the property, then I had no further obligations to the funeral man. However, if I did acquire the property, then I would have a guaranteed tenant. With my rental from this property guaranteed at $30,000 per annum, and using a conservative cap rate of 12.5%, the property had to be worth $240,000 to me ($30,000 divided by 12.5%).

I ended up acquiring the property for a net price of $170,000. The bank initially appraised the property at $240,000 and gave me a mortgage with a loan-value ratio of 67%. In this manner, I borrowed $160,000, so that I only had to put in $10,000 of my own cash. My rental income was $30,000, and since the tenants paid most of the outgoings, my only real expense was the mortgage interest, which was initially $15,000. In summary, therefore, for an investment of only $10,000 cash, I had a net income of $15,000 per annum indexed for inflation, and I had created $70,000 of equity tax free out of thin air.

The initial increase in value was $70,000 as we have just seen. However, we subsequently did a few more things to the building (see for instance item number 56), and within a couple of months, the funeral parlor appraised at $280,000, fully $110,000 more than I paid for it. Would $110,000 make you feel a bit less squeamish about a funeral parlor?

Finding a tenant for vacant commercial space is such a lucrative approach, that I have made a specialty out of it. Most people, when they come across vacant space, dismiss it as a bad proposition with zero returns, and move on to look for something with a tenant in place. I mull it over in my mind, and try to figure out a way of attracting a tenant to this property. If I can, then I will massively increase its value.

81. *Create value from vacant land.*

We saw above that when it comes to commercial property, the value is not so much determined by the intrinsic value of the components (the land itself and the buildings) but rather by the income generating capacity of the property.

Thus, when it comes to vacant land, there is little income to be derived. Often, the only solution for vacant land is to let grass grow, and then to rent the land out to horse owners for grazing. Needless to say, the rentals will hardly finance the winter storage of your yacht at Cannes.

However, vacant land can be put to great use if you use your creativity. Find out what there is a demand for. Put up a high-security fence, and suddenly you have the perfect place for a trucking company to park its vehicles overnight, or for a rental car company to store its surplus vehicles during the quiet season. Throw on a prefabricated office, or a mobile trailer of some sort, and you then can lease out the space to an airport parking operator who stores clients' cars securely and shuttles their owners to and from the airport.

82. *Erect a parking building.*

The value of commercial space is often quoted as being so many dollars *per square foot* or *per square meter*. When it comes to office space, the value is further differentiated by whether or not there are adequate parking facilities. For instance, it may be expected that there are at least four spaces per thousand square feet of office space, in which case the rental may be, say, $24 per square foot. If there are only one or two spaces per thousand square feet, then the rental may be only $15 per square foot.

The more you can think laterally, the more you will see this situation as an opportunity of proportions unparalleled in the residential real estate world. For example, I once looked at a 36-story office building in downtown Fort Worth,

Texas. With a paltry number of onsite parking spaces, the rentals came in at around $16 psf. However, by acquiring a six-story parking garage nearby and assigning the garage to the 36-story tower, suddenly the rentals could be raised to around $22 psf. The differential, when multiplied by the total square footage of the building, came in at around $2.4 million per annum. Multiplying that by the cap rate (capitalization rate) or a generous 10%, and the value of the property went up by around $24 million, or many times more than the cost of the parking garage.

In Japan, with its chronic shortage of space, they have come up with creative ways of parking many cars in a very small area. A common system is to use a Paternoster-like elevator, where cars are driven onto a platform, and then rotated up into the parking building (it's a bit like a Ferris wheel, but not circular—imagine buckets on a vertical conveyor belt). In this manner, they can store up to 52 vehicles on a footprint the width of two and a half cars, one car length deep, and about 26 car-heights tall. When you drop your car off, you get a plastic card corresponding to the "bucket" on which your car is driven. When you return, you insert the card, and your car is rotated back to the bottom position for you to drive off in it.

83. *Make the office pleasant.*

There is a very simple and straightforward way to improve the value of any industrial real estate you may have. Remember that with almost all commercial real estate, the value is generally determined by capitalizing the rental income. Thus, if you can double the rental income, you can generally double the worth of the real estate.

Most industrial property has a combination of warehouses, storage facilities, paint shops, workshops, and a variety of other buildings specifically designed and equipped to perform tasks of manufacturing, design, repair, or servicing. However, one thing they almost all have in common is an office for the manager. Now, guess who gets to inspect an industrial building to see if it is suitable for the company to rent. This person is generally none other than the manager who will occupy the office. So, all you need to do is make the office as pleasant as practical. Most managers at industrial plants are used to dingy offices, with no carpets, coffee making facilities, music, or amenities. So, if you can paint the offices well, put in a nice carpet, add some great lighting, and add a number of features that you feel a typical manager of such a premise will not be used to, then by the time he gets to inspect your premises, he will be sold on renting them, even if the rent is somewhat higher than comparable areas elsewhere, or even if the rest of the building is not quite as well suited to their business as other premises.

84. *Turn the building into a huge advertisement.*

If you own a large commercial building, and it is vacant, then do not just put up a little one-foot by two-foot sign somewhere along the half-mile perimeter of the property. Make a huge canvas (reusable!) banner advertisement that you hang on all sides of the building advertising the fact that your premises are for rent. If it costs $8,000 to make such a monstrous, multicolored banner, and you manage to secure a tenant 5 months earlier than you otherwise would have, at $12,000 rent per month, will it have been a good investment of $8,000?

85. *Sell the naming rights to your building.*

Few people realize that when a building has a name (such as Kodak House or the IBM Tower), usually a tenant has paid for the right to attach his name to the building. In other words, if you own a large commercial building, and it has not been named, auction the rights to name that building under a lease arrangement. If it already has a name, check the rent-review and renewal clauses on the lease. In major cities, naming rights can bring in hundreds of thousands of dollars a year in income.

86. *Rent out space for cell-phone towers.*

Another source of extra income for very little effort is to lease out space on the roof of your buildings for the place-ment of cell-phone towers, microwave repeater stations, satellite communication dishes, weather stations, and pollu-tion monitoring systems. Don't just wait for the relevant par-ties to track you down and contact you. Write letters to these parties mentioning buildings you own in their region, tell all your property managers about it, and put the word out. A satellite dish or cell-phone tower may only generate $6,000 a year in income, but that is a great return on three phone calls and two letters.

87. *Rent out billboard space.*

I once came across a long, narrow building that had been va-cant for years because of its awkward shape. While it was po-sitioned parallel to a busy freeway, access to the freeway was many miles away. No one could figure out what to do with it, as everyone was focused on doing something useful with the space inside the narrow building. The only thing I could think of was a rope factory. That is until I reminded myself that the value of a commercial property is largely deter-mined by the income that it can generate, and this income does not have to be generated by leasing out the inside of the building.

What we did was rent out space on the side of the building facing the busy freeway for a huge billboard. The rental from that alone more than covered the holding costs of the building. Later, the inside of the building was converted to storage units.

88. *Convert existing buildings to storage units.*

As our lives become more sophisticated and we acquire ever more gadgets, appliances, devices, and just stuff, our possessions are spilling out from our homes into storage units. I can hardly remember any storage units when I was young, but these days, driving around just about any city will reveal signs for all manner of storage facilities, from the ultra-secure to airconditioned, and ranging in size from a few square feet for document storage to hundreds of square feet for household goods.

Do some homework. If there is a shortage of storage units in a particular area, then consider building some on that vacant land of yours, or convert an existing empty or underutilized building to serve as storage units. The beauty of storage units is that tenants always pay in advance, and if by chance they do end up falling behind in rent, then simply adding your padlock to the door generally ensures that they willing pay up any backlog of rent!

89. *Change the size of the rental units.*

Even if a commercial property is fully leased, it may not be a very efficient way of filling the space. For instance, you may have a large, 10,000 square-foot warehouse leased at $3 per square foot. It may be difficult to retain tenants, simply because there is not much demand in that area for such large warehouses. In this case you could be much better off dividing the warehouse into much smaller units, perhaps 5 units of 2,000 square feet each, or even 20 units of 500 square feet each. If market rentals per square foot for this size warehouse are around $5, then you will have nearly doubled the value of your property.

90. *Let's build five storage garages.*

The first example in this book with the carport is real enough, but the concept also works for much larger projects. Here is the only other example in this book that I also described in some detail in *Real Estate Riches*.

I own a block of shops that are butted up to the sidewalk, but in the back there was a lot of vacant land. It was continually being overgrown by weeds, and the tenants tended to store their rubbish there. I was after a creative solution. This is what I did:

I found out that rentals on storage garages were running at around $40 a week. My vacant land could just accommodate five garages, for a total of $200 per week, or just over $10,000 per year. I knew that capitalization rates on commercial properties in the area were hovering around 10%, so theoretically the extra rental of $10,000 per annum would increase the capital value of the property by around $100,000. All that remained to be done was to figure out what the garages would cost to build.

The quote came in at $33,000. Once again I faced a choice. Either I could build the garages for $33,000 cash, and enjoy a healthy 30% return on capital ($10,000 annual income divided by $33,000 capital outlay). Or I could have the garages built, get a new appraisal, and borrow against the extra $100,000 of equity. At 70%, that would put $37,000 of tax-free money in my pocket, and still give me an annual income (indexed for inflation) of around $3,000 ($10,000 rental income less say 10% interest on a $70,000 mortgage).

Again, the point is, if you are in such a situation, why would you not do it? It's not as if you have to build the carport yourself, let alone the garages. In the latter case, I simply made a series of phone calls: to several contractors for quotes, to an architect for some drawings, to an appraiser to get the appraisal done, and to the bank to arrange a new mortgage. It is not difficult. In fact, I would go so far as to confess that it is not even particularly mentally stimulating. But it sure is lucrative!

As soon as you learn about the carport concept, I am sure that you will never see a residential investment property that does not have a carport in the same light again. In fact, when such a property is on the market, others will tend to see it in a negative light (it doesn't even have a carport!), which will further decrease interest in that property. That in turn will reduce the expectations of sale price for the seller. After a while, you will hear yourself saying: "Great!" when a property doesn't have a carport or garage.

The same applies to a property with some spare vacant land. You will wonder: "What else can I put up here that will generate income?" After all, you do not have to pay for the land!

Of course, you have to check that the carports and garages conform to local regulations in terms of site coverage (sometimes, not all of the area of a property may be covered in buildings) and other restrictions. But on average your efforts will be well rewarded.

Section 3

Upmarket Homes

While the ideas in Section One can generally be applied to just about any home that you may end up acquiring as an investment, I want to share some of the things you can do to more up-market homes. While a smaller proportion of high-end homes may be owned by investors (the cash flow returns tend to be lower than with cheaper homes), if you do own or end up owning some of these as investments, then the ideas that follow may give you far greater returns than what you would expect to gain from implementing the ideas in the first section.

91. *Put in a helipad.*

My simplest example for upmarket homes is to build a helipad. The mere word helipad evokes images of great wealth, but the truth is that a helipad need be nothing more than a solid slab of concrete, with the letter H painted on it, which is done to prevent your guests from thinking that maybe the slab in the middle of your expansive front lawn is an unfinished basketball court, and to help pilots identify where they may drop in for afternoon tea.

I am sure you will agree that the slab of concrete will not cost much. When the concrete has set, however, you can boast that you can receive visitors by helicopter. When they now write about this property in the *Robb Report*, or talk about it on *Entertainment Tonight*, the mere mention of a helipad will increase the perceived value by tens of thousands of dollars. Not bad for a couple of hundred dollars worth of concrete.

92. *Trickle chargers and chocks for the classic car collection.*

Now that we are working on our expensive mansion, let's talk about the 5-car garage. For an appraisal report to be able to say that the property has a 5-car garage is of course quite something in and of itself. However, what would you think if the wording could read: "the 5-car garage comes equipped with fives sets of trickle chargers and chocks to keep a private collection of classic cars in perfect condition." Many men, even if they have never owned a classic car in their lives, harbor some deep seated desire to do so in the future. The effect on the value of the real estate can be enormous.

93. *Install a home spa.*

While it may be difficult to justify a home spa in a cheaper rental unit, in an expensive home the addition of a $15,000 home spa complete with pumps, heater, filters, and adjacent mini-bar may bump up the value of the real estate by $50,000. The point is to do your homework, and then give it a go.

94. *Put in a swimming pool.*

Adding a swimming pool may make sense as well. While in most parts of the world, a swimming pool is still considered a luxury item, there are many regions where a pool is considered a necessity (alright, I did say *considered*). Thus, if your house is one of the very few that does not sport one, then the house's value will be downgraded without one.

95. *Remove a swimming pool.*

Before you think that I want to have it both ways, I am not talking about removing a single swimming pool, but rather removing a second swimming pool. Friends of mine in Phoenix, Arizona have what could be described as a sizable house with a big chunk of land. The house boasted not just one, but two swimming pools. The pools got a lot of use, not by my friends, but by an extended family of ducks who had decided to take up residence in the pool, giving my friends the added bonus of free fertilizer gunk. The cost of maintaining two pools was ridiculous, especially given that you can only swim in one at a time. They decided to remove one, and have never looked back since. They are now trying to figure out what to do with the tennis court that they never use. As Robert Kiyosaki says, there are two kinds of problems: problems that come about from having too little money, and problems that come about from having too much money. All other things being equal, the latter kind is still preferable!

96. *Rise to the occasion.*

It is somewhat sad but true that great wealth seems to come to us when we have a diminished ability to really enjoy it. As a kid in Dunedin, it used to make me cringe, while I pedaled home from school on my bicycle, to see an immaculately dressed older man with silver white hair putter along in fourth gear at 20 mph in a brand-new Mercedes Benz sports coupe. I felt a swap was in order, as at least he couldn't harm the bicycle by going too slowly.

If it is true that we accumulate wealth during our lives, then in theory at least, we should have more wealth as we get older and become less mobile. That is why for top-end multistory homes, adding an elevator can make it appealing to a large body of fabulously wealthy individuals who would otherwise not consider your property because of their reluctance to negotiate stairs.

Most elevators installed in a home environment are hydraulic, which are somewhat slower than conventional motorized elevators, but much cheaper and easier to install as a retrofit. In any case, a $10,000 elevator can easily add $40,000 to the value of the property.

97. *Build a Multi-Media Theater.*

Not too many years ago, the cost of fitting a multimedia theater to a home was measured in the tens of thousands of dollars. Today, with falling prices of home theater hardware including large flat-panel displays and projection units, you get a lot more value for your money.

Assume you have a million-dollar house on a street of similar homes, and you have just installed a multimedia theater. If prospective tenants were to visit your property, and all the other properties they inspected did not have such a theater, do you think you may have an advantage? Imagine if for 10% extra in rent compared with other properties, they could have your theater, complete with a collection of 50 DVDs (heck, they only cost you a few hundred dollars). Might they go for it? You will recoup the cost of installing the theater through the extra rental in no time, and the value of the property will have gone up dramatically. Again, why would you not do it?

98. *Install a video security system.*

A video security system may include multiple video cameras with one or two monitoring stations—perhaps one monitoring station in the home office, and one near the master bedroom. Cameras may be placed at the front gates (to see who has pulled up and has pushed the intercom button), at the front door, and at strategic locations around the property. The fact that a video security system is in place may be worth a lot more to high net worth individuals than the cost to you of installing the system.

99. *Electric and remote-controlled entrance gates.*

We have all seen them: entrance gates that can be activated from within your car, or from within the house if you want to let guests in. Well, if you don't have them, check out the cost of installing them. It is a classic example of something where the perceived value is much greater than the cost of implementation.

100. *Install a rotating platform in the driveway.*

Many people have difficulty backing a car out of a driveway. One solution for our upscale home is to install a large, circular platform that is level with the driveway. The vehicle is backed out of the garage onto this platform, and then the platform can be rotated by remote control, so that the vehicle ends up facing the direction of intended travel. Once again, do not question whether you would be sissy enough to need such a contraption. Stay focused on the outcome, namely to create more equity (and therefore net worth) for yourself than the cost of implementing the creation. If it costs $5,500 to install such a platform, but the value of the property goes up by $20,000, then I would suggest it is a good trade-off.

Seen in isolation, each of these upmarket-home ideas may seem frivolous, the unnecessary excesses of the super-rich. However, compared with a "standard" upmarket home, if yours has a helipad, trickle chargers for the classic cars, a home spa, swimming pool, hydraulic elevator, multimedia theater, video security system, electric and remote-controlled entrance gates, and a rotating platform in the driveway, it is not unreasonable that if the standard homes sold for $1,500,000, yours could sell for $1,700,000. Assuming you could build the features described for around $100,000, then here is a quick $100,000 to be made. Why would you not do it?

101. *Saving the best for last.*

We have already arrived at number 101. There is nothing magical or deterministic about the number one-hundred-and-one. We could easily go on and dream up (and implement) another 101 ideas. In fact, I invite you to go to my web site to submit ideas that I may have overlooked here—these postings can be viewed by all, so that this can be a resource of ongoing ideas for real estate investors. However, for this book, I have saved my most creative and obtuse idea for last.

So far, we have considered things that you can do to massively increase the value of your real estate without spending much money. However, in each of the preceding 100 cases, the money we have spent has been spent *on our own property.*

Imagine you own a house on which you have made all the improvements that you think are warranted. In other words, you have implemented all the desired improvements. What is there left to do?

Well, imagine that the houses on either side of yours are in a horrible state of repair. In particular, the paint is so faded on these houses that it is difficult to determine exactly which color was most recently applied to them.

What if you were to paint these two houses? Would it cost you money? Sure it would, although if you didn't want your benevolence to be total, you could seek a subsidy from their respective owners. But even if they did not want to contribute, and you went ahead and painted them anyway, do you think you might create some goodwill with your neighbors? You'd better believe it. They will think you are the greatest. However, the exercise will not have been totally without self-interest, as any appraiser, whether he would admit it or not, would be inclined to think more of your house when it is one of several great looking properties, than when it is a rose among a bed of thorns.

Of course this idea is not restricted to painting the

houses on either side of your own. You could mow the lawns, remove rubbish, repair fences, and fix letter boxes of the neighboring houses. I am reminded of one of my early experiences with real estate:

I once owned a restaurant in beautiful Cass Bay, New Zealand. The building was in a wooded area, with trees and shrubs all around. On the street side, there was a bus-stop shelter provided by the local city council. The paint that had not been worn off by the elements had been subjected to the talents of the local graffiti artists. The whole thing was an eyesore of monumental proportions that inevitably dragged the whole feel of the surrounding properties down. I badgered the city council endlessly to have it painted. I reminded them that as a property investor with numerous pieces of real estate to my name in the area, I made more than the average contributions through my property taxes to their salaries, luncheons, paid leave, and perks, and could they not please me and everyone else in Cass Bay by sending someone out with half a bucket of paint to paint the hideous thing. After two years of unfulfilled promises, I decided to take matters into my own hands.

With some trepidation borne from feeling I was doing something wrong, I set out at dusk to do what I felt I had been paying the council to do, but on which they had reneged. The deed took all of 35 minutes, and the results were spectacular. Now, for the first time, the look of the bus-stop shelter accurately reflected the style and feel of the surroundings, including my restaurant.

I never received any thanks from the council, and to this day they probably do not know that it had been painted. But, from that day on, strange things started to happen. The restaurant became more popular. Diners commented that the food tasted better. My tenant, the restaurateur, claimed that there had been an improvement in the weather. There were fewer flies that summer. Locals whistled as they walked past the restaurant. Children played on the front lawn. Oh, and I nearly forgot, the appraiser increased his estimate of the real estate value by $40,000, even though nothing had been done to the property itself. Not bad for half a pail of old paint and 35 minutes work spent on someone else's bus-stop shelter.

In closing...

I hope to have whetted your appetite just a little bit for the sorts of things you can do to have a dramatic effect on the value of a property without spending much money. And remember, this list is not exhaustive. We could still fit vertical blinds, take out a fireplace, install a wood stove, put in ceiling fans, blow out a wall, or subdivide a huge room. The optimal mix of improvements will depend on the state of the local market, the condition of the house, the specific condition of the items being considered for replacement, and the local culture.

After reading this book, I am hoping that if someone shouts out loud: "Property without a carport or garage!" you will immediately recognize that there is an opportunity here to put money in your pocket. In a similar vein, every time that I inspect a property, a voice inside my head blurts out all the things that I can do to massively increase the value of the property I am looking at.

In that sense, when I look at a property, it is a different property from when you look at it. Of course physically it is still one and the same property, but we each bring with us a different set of experiences, ideas, and daring, so that a property that I think will not work for me, may well work

handsomely for you, and vice versa.

The secret is to do your homework, get the courage of your convictions, and then dare to try. You will either win or learn. And you never learn less.

The thing I love about real estate is that you are truly limited only by your own imagination. I hope this book has given you some ideas. But at some stage, I encourage you to stop reading and start doing!

Successful investing!
Dolf de Roos

About the Author

 Dr. Dolf de Roos began investing in real estate as an undergraduate student. Despite going on to earn a Ph.D. in Electrical and Electronic Engineering from the University of Canterbury, Dolf increasingly focused on his flair for investing, which has enabled him to have never had a job. He has, however, invested in many classes of real estate (residential, commercial, industrial, hospitality, and specialist) all over the world.

Today he is the chairman of the public company Property Ventures Limited, an innovative real estate investment company whose stated mission is to massively increase stockholders' worth. Over the years, Dolf was cajoled into sharing his investment strategies, and he has run seminars on the Psychology of Creating Wealth and on Real Estate Investing throughout North America, Australia, New Zealand, Asia, the Middle East, and Europe since the 1980s.

Beyond sharing his investment philosophy and strategies with tens of thousands of investors (beginners as well as seasoned experts), Dolf has also trained real estate agents,

written and published numerous books on property, and introduced computer software designed to analyze and manage properties quickly and efficiently. He often speaks at investors' conferences, realtors' conventions, and his own international seminars, and regularly takes part in radio shows and television debates. Born in New Zealand, raised in Australia, New Zealand, and Europe, Dolf, with six languages up his sleeve, offers a truly global perspective on the surprisingly lucrative wealth-building opportunities of real estate. Dolf has shared the platform with his friend Robert Kiyosaki for many years and is one of his select *Rich Dad's Advisors*™.

To find out what you can learn from Dolf's willingness to share his knowledge about creating wealth through real estate, and to receive his free monthly newsletter, please visit his web site at www.dolfderoos.com.

How to take advantage of resources available to create wealth through real estate.

With real estate, as with most other activities in life, you cannot hope to learn all you need to know by reading one book once. Although real estate is far more stable, consistent, and dependable than most other financial activities, keeping up with trends and ahead of the competition is imperative. Read many books on the subject (the book you don't read cannot help you!), attend seminars, talk with other investors, and dream up your own ideas to try out in the marketplace.

Success leaves clues! We have a number of resources to help both aspiring and seasoned investors. Please visit our web site www.dolfderoos.com to find out about our:

- Books
- Tape Sets and CDs
- Software
- Mentoring programs
- Seminar schedules
- New products, services, and events

Finally, remember that contrary to the saying *knowledge is power*, it is only applied knowledge that is power. It is not enough to know a lot about real estate—to achieve real estate riches, you must put the theories into action. It is the difference between being interested and being committed.

Subscribe to our free monthly newsletter.

We trust that the resources available on our web site www.dolfderoos.com will empower you and propel you on your way to not needing (or wanting!) a job, thanks to real estate.

The next 101 ideas to massively increase the value of your real estate without spending much money.

Do you think Dolf has left off some brilliant ways of adding tremendous value to a property without spending much money? Visit our web site www.dolfderoos.com to submit your suggestion (anonymously or with your name), and check out ideas that others have submitted.

On the web site we also have photographic examples of ideas in this book that have been implemented. Check them out to gain confidence or inspiration.

Finally, always remember that ideas are funny little things: They only work if you do. Although real estate has one of the highest conversion rates of effort into dollars, at some stage you have to stop reading and start doing!

Successful investing!